DIFFICULT & DANGEROUS

Secret Missions

ALEX BROWN

FRANKLIN WATTS

An Appleseed Editions book

First published in 2008 by Franklin Watts

Franklin Watts
338 Euston Road, London NW1 3BH

Franklin Watts Australia
Level 17/207 Kent St, Sydney, NSW 2000

2008 Appleseed Editions

Appleseed Editions Ltd
Well House, Friars Hill, Guestling, East Sussex TN35 4ET

Created by Q2A Media
Series Editor: Jean Coppendale
Book Editor: Paul Manning
Senior Art Designers: Ashita Murgai, Nishant Mudgal
Designer: Shilpi Sarkar
Picture Researcher: Lalit Dalal
Line Artists: Amit Tayal, Sibi N.D
Illustrators: Aadil Ahmed Siddiqui, Amir Khan, Kusum Kala, Sanyogita Lal

ISBN 978 0 7496 8053 4

Dewey classification: 327.12

All words in **bold** can be found in the glossary on page 30.

Website information is correct at time of going to press. However, the publishers cannot
accept liability for any information or links found on third-party websites.

A CIP catalogue for this book is available from the British Library.

Picture credits
t=top b=bottom c=centre l=left r=right m=middle
Cover: Q2A Media
Taolmor: 4t, Movieposter.com: 4bl, Utah Images / NASA / Alamy: 4br, Prints and Photographs Division/ Library of
Congress: 6t, 6b, North Wind Picture Archives/ Alamy: 7t, Prints and Photographs Division/ Library of Congress: 9b,
10t, Carmen Negroni: 10b, Pictorial Press Ltd / Alamy: 11, Jersey War Tunnels: 13t, Emma Holmwood: 14,
Ira Nowinski/ Corbis: 15t, IWM: 15b, Tim Ockenden/ PA Archive/ PA Photos: 16, Bettmann/ Corbis: 17,
U.S. National Archives: 18, 19t, 19b, Bettmann/ Corbis: 20t, CIA: 20b, Prints and Photographs Division/ Library of
Congress: 21t, William Campbell/ Sygma/ Corbis: 21b, Don Rutledge/ Stanley Leary: 22, Prints and Photographs
Division/ Library of Congress: 23l, R.C. Hickman: 23m, Jack Moebes/ Corbis: 23r, Af.mil: 27t,
Time & Life Pictures/ Getty Images: 23b, Bettmann/ Corbis: 29t, 29b.

Printed in Hong Kong

Franklin Watts is a division of Hachette Children's Books

Contents

SPIES AND SECRET AGENTS

In books and films, spies often lead glamorous and exciting lives, but the reality is often very different. Ever since ancient times, spies and secret agents have carried out difficult and dangerous missions to find out information about their enemies.

Spies in wartime

In times of war, spies play a vital part in finding out information about the enemy's plans and deceiving them about when and where to expect an attack. Some of the most dangerous wartime missions have been carried out by **double agents** - men and women who pretend to be working for one side while secretly passing information to the enemy. Unlike prisoners of war who are protected by the **Geneva Convention**, a spy who is unmasked or captured can expect no mercy.

*Spies often use **codes** and **ciphers** to prevent their messages being intercepted by the enemy. This wartime agent is sending a message in **Morse code** via a radio transmitter hidden in a suitcase*

Spies in history

In the 4th century BC, Alexander the Great used spies to track enemy troop movements and find the best marching routes for his massive armies. Spies also helped the Mongol leader Genghis Khan (1162–1227) to conquer most of Asia. Khan's agents were local men who could move around freely and collect **intelligence** without arousing suspicion.

The Macedonian emperor Alexander the Great

Actor Daniel Craig as the fictional spy James Bond in the film Casino Royale

Spying today

Today, much spying is done by satellite cameras high in the sky. But down on the ground, human spies still lead dangerous lives. Some work like burglars to steal military secrets. Others try to win their enemy's trust by posing as a friend or ally. By passing secrets to the other side, spies can win or lose wars and change the course of history.

Satellite cameras in space are widely used by intelligence agencies and can provide amazingly accurate pictures of objects and people on the ground. Some can even distinguish between civilians and military personnel

'WE NEVER SLEEP'
The story of the Pinkerton Detective Agency

Founded in 1850, Pinkerton's National Detective Agency was one of the first organizations to use paid investigators to track down criminals and bring them to justice. Pinkerton himself solved many crimes, often using methods that are still used by law-enforcement officers today.

Born in Scotland in 1819, Allan Pinkerton emigrated to the USA in 1842 to escape arrest for his political views. He founded the Pinkerton National Detective Agency in 1850, after working as Chicago's first full-time police detective. As case followed successful case, the Pinkerton Agency became a household name. At the height of its powers in the 1850s and 60s, the agency employed more agents than the entire standing army of the USA!

Pinkerton agents of the 1870s: Allan Pinkerton's son William (centre) with railroad special agents Pat Connell (left) and Sam Finley (right)

On the trail of the train robbers

One of Pinkerton's most famous early cases was that of the Adams Express Railway mail service. In 1858 the company lost about $50,000 – a huge sum in those days – in a series of train robberies. Suspecting an inside job, Pinkerton ordered his agents to follow John Maroney, an Adams employee who was in charge of sealing the boxes of money before they were loaded on board the trains.

Stolen money

For weeks, Pinkerton's men **shadowed** Maroney and his wife. Eventually an agent posing as a criminal gained Maroney's trust and tricked his wife into revealing the stolen money, hidden in a trunk in the cellar of their house. She was immediately arrested and the Maroneys charged with the robbery.

Train robberies, bank hold-ups, gunfights and the general lawlessness of the Wild West brought Pinkerton and his agents a steady stream of work in 1860s America

PINKERTON'S NATIONAL DETECTIVE AGENCY.

We never sleep.

The first 'private eye'

The term 'private eye' goes back to the Pinkerton agency's motto, 'We Never Sleep', and its logo of an ever-watchful eye. The Pinkerton-style private eye later became a popular figure in many classic films and detective stories.

Bodyguard to the president

Early in his career, Pinkerton came into contact with a young lawyer named Abraham Lincoln. The two became good friends. In 1860, Lincoln decided to run for the presidency. Lincoln was openly opposed to slavery and many white people hated him for this. Pinkerton knew that such hatred would put Lincoln's life in danger and agreed to act as Lincoln's personal security adviser.

In 1861, Pinkerton received a tip-off that members of a pro-slavery secret society were plotting to assassinate Lincoln while he travelled to his inauguration in Washington. Pinkerton immediately contacted Lincoln and warned him to change his route. The following evening, trains specially chartered by Pinkerton secretly carried Lincoln back to Washington. By morning, when the assassins were expecting him to arrive at Baltimore, Lincoln was hundreds of miles away and out of danger.

Civil war

When civil war divided the USA, Lincoln once more turned to Pinkerton for help - this time to gather intelligence for the Unionist army. Unfortunately, Pinkerton knew very little about military espionage, and his agents were often careless. On 17 September 1862, 2,100 Unionist soldiers died at the Battle of Antietam, largely as a result of poor intelligence, and Pinkerton resigned.

Warned of an attempt on Lincoln's life, Pinkerton and his agents escort him to the safety of a waiting train

Grey areas were not states before or during the Civil War

- Confederate/Union boundary
- Union states
- Union states which permitted slavery
- Confederate States

STATES OF THE UNION

CONFEDERATE STATES

Atlantic Ocean

MEXICO

Gulf of Mexico

The American Civil War (1861–5) was fought between northern states which supported the Union (the 'States of the Union') and opposed slavery, and twelve southern states, which tried to break away to form a separate Confederate States of America. After much fierce fighting, the Union was restored and slavery was abolished.

Pinkerton (left) photographed with President Lincoln (centre) and General John McClernand shortly before the Battle of Antietam in 1862

On the outlaw trail

In the years following the Civil War, Pinkerton and his men investigated cases involving everything from **counterfeiting** and **wiretapping** to robbery and murder. They also brought to justice many of the most notorious outlaws of the Wild West, including Jesse James, Butch Cassidy *(right)* and the Sundance Kid, 'Black Jack' Tom Ketcham, Hillary Farrington and the Reno brothers.

In 1884, Pinkerton suffered a stroke, and the great Chicago fire destroyed the company's headquarters. Soon after, Allan Pinkerton died and his sons William and Robert took over as principals of the company. Today, the Pinkerton organization is still one of America's leading security companies.

As well as pioneering the use of **fingerprinting**, Pinkerton was the first to make use of **mugshots** and 'wanted' posters to catch dangerous criminals. Pictured above is the outlaw Robert E. Parker, better known as Butch Cassidy

Could YOU be a private eye?

Before the days of CCTV and electronic bugging devices, private investigators had to rely on eyes and ears and quick wits.

How observant are YOU?

Relying just on memory, make up a 'wanted' poster for someone you know. Include their age, height, colouring and any distinguishing marks, and describe what they were wearing when you last saw them. If you like, draw criminal-style 'mugshots' to show what they look like from the front and the side.

A 'wanted' poster for the outlaws Frank and Jesse James

HEROINE OF THE RESISTANCE

The story of Violette Szabo

*In 1940, Western Europe was under the control of Nazi Germany. But small bands of **Resistance** fighters still waged a secret war against the occupying German forces. One of the bravest was the British secret service agent Violette Szabo (1921-45).*

Szabo was born in Paris to a French mother and an English father but spent her early years in London. In 1940, she married Etienne Szabo, a captain in the French Foreign Legion. When Etienne was killed fighting the Germans in North Africa in 1942, Violette was devastated. Only months earlier she had given birth to their first child, a baby daughter.

'Dangerous work'

Determined to avenge her husband's death, Violette wrote to the authorities to offer her services. An interview followed with the British **Special Operations Executive** (SOE), and within days Violette found herself being trained for 'dangerous work' in enemy-occupied France.

Beautiful, courageous – and deadly, Violette Szabo's special talents made her an ideal candidate for the SOE. A fluent French speaker, she was also an excellent shot with a gun. According to friends, she was even banned from fairground shooting galleries because she always hit the target!

11

Behind enemy lines

The key role of the SOE was to train agents to carry out **sabotage** and **subversion** behind enemy lines. That meant blowing up bridges, railway lines and weapons dumps and doing all they could to make life difficult and unpleasant for the Nazis. Violette Szabo knew that the life of an SOE agent was lonely, dangerous - and often short. But she was prepared. Within a few weeks she had completed her training and was ready for her first mission. On 5 April 1944, she was flown across the English Channel and dropped by parachute on the outskirts of a small town near Cherbourg.

Occupied France in 1944, showing the location of Violette Szabo's two secret missions

Violette and her comrades in the French Resistance destroy a bridge used by German forces in Occupied France

An SOE agent's training

SOE agents like Violette Szabo were trained in large country houses in England or remote parts of Scotland. Men and women recruits learned how to kill quickly and silently with their bare hands; how to disguise themselves; how to derail a train with explosives – even how to get out of a pair of handcuffs with a piece of thin wire. After parachute training and gruelling outdoor survival tests, they were ready for action.

Gun
Knife
Forged papers
Binoculars
Map and compass
Flashlight
Secret radio transmitter

Above: A typical SOE agent's equipment checklist. SOE agents also carried a suicide pill to swallow if they fell into enemy hands. None is believed to have used it.
Right: Violette Szabo's automatic pistol

A thorn in the side of the Nazis

Violette's task was to make contact with former members of a local Resistance 'cell' and help them regroup to fight the Nazis. Violette more than fulfilled her mission. Soon she was leading the group in blowing up bridges and disrupting the German supply routes. She also supplied information which helped **Allied** bombers to carry out major raids on German weapons factories. After six weeks she returned to London. She had passed her first test with flying colours.

13

Captured by the Gestapo

A month after her first venture into enemy territory, Violette Szabo returned to Occupied France with three other British agents. Her mission this time was to unite local Resistance groups and carry out sabotage operations around Limoges. On 9 June, Szabo received orders to make contact with Jacques Poirier, one of the leaders of the Resistance. The next day she set off for the rendezvous by car, accompanied by two members of the local **Maquis**. The trio had not gone far when they were attacked by a German unit. Her two companions escaped, but after a fierce gun battle Violette was captured by the Germans.

Capture by the Germans was an ever-present risk for SOE agents and Resistance fighters. Countless numbers were tortured by the Gestapo or ended their lives in German prisons and concentration camps

A prisoner in Ravensbruck

Szabo was taken to **Gestapo** headquarters in Paris. Despite cruel torture, she refused to talk. After days of interrogation, she was transferred to the Ravensbruck concentration camp in Germany *(right)*. For five long months her ordeal continued. Finally one day, she was taken out into a yard where she was made to kneel down, and killed with a single bullet to the back of her neck. She was 23 years old.

Medal of courage

On 17 December 1946, after the war ended, Violette Szabo became one of only four women to be awarded the **George Cross**. Her daughter Tania received the decoration on her behalf. She was also awarded the **Croix de Guerre** by the French government. After the war, her life became the subject of a successful film, *Carve Her Name With Pride*, starring Virginia McKenna.

The crematorium of Ravensbruck concentration camp in northern Germany, where Violette was taken after her interrogation by the Gestapo. Living conditions in the camp were appalling, and the treatment of inmates unimaginably brutal. Out of more than 130,000 female prisoners who passed though its gates, only 40,000 survived

The George Cross is Britain's highest award for civilian gallantry

Could YOU use codes and ciphers?

1 During their training, all SOE agents were taught how to send and receive messages in code. How good are YOU at using codes? Try and decode the message below. *Clue:* Substitute the numbers 1 with A, 2 with B, 3 with C and so on and so on.

23-5-12-12 / 4-15-14-5! 25-15-21 / 8-1-22-5 / 3-18-1-3-11-5-4 / 20-8-5 / 3-15-4-5.

2 Another type of code is a book cipher. This works by replacing the words of the message with numbers which tell the person receiving the message where to find the same words in a chosen book or text.

Try it with a friend. Violette Szabo based her book cipher on a favourite poem. What book or poem will you choose?

Answer Well done! You have cracked the code.

15

MASTER OF DECEPTION

The life and times of Dusan 'Dusko' Popov

During World War II, Dusan 'Dusko' Popov (1912–81) played a dangerous double game. Outwardly he was a wealthy Serbian businessman with a taste for the high life. Secretly, he was working as a double agent for both the British and German intelligence services.

Early in the war Popov had been recruited by the German military intelligence service to **infiltrate MI5**, the British secret service. Unknown to the Germans, Popov's real loyalties lay with Britain. Using his business activities as a cover, Popov made regular visits to Portugal, where he passed information approved by MI5 to his German masters. The Germans paid him well for his efforts, but after the war, Popov was awarded the **OBE** - for his services to Britain!

*In wartime Europe, travel was very restricted, but flights to **neutral** countries such as Portugal, Spain or Switzerland (shown in grey above) were still permitted. As a foreign national, Popov could make regular trips to Portugal without arousing suspicion*

'Dusko' Popov is widely believed to be the real-life model for fictional spy James Bond. Like Bond, Popov loved to stay at the best hotels, ate at top restaurants, visited smart casinos and enjoyed the company of beautiful women

Popov's warning ignored

In August 1941, Popov's German **spymasters** sent him to the USA with orders to gather information about Pearl Harbor, a key US naval base. As soon as he arrived, he secretly contacted the **FBI** to warn them that the US fleet could be in danger. But FBI boss J. Edgar Hoover ignored his warning.

What Hoover did not realize was that the Germans were collecting information for their ally - Japan. His mistake proved costly. On 7 December 1941, Japanese planes bombed Pearl Harbor, crippling the naval fleet and killing 2,300 Americans.

The surprise Japanese air attack on Pearl Harbor was a disaster for the USA, but also led ultimately to the defeat of Nazi Germany. Following the attack by Japan, it was inevitable that the USA would enter the war on the Allied side

D-Day deception

By the early months of 1944, Allied troops were assembling in vast numbers on the south coast of England, ready to begin the assault on Hitler's forces in Europe. The date set for the assault was 6 June, codenamed 'D-Day'. But in order for the invasion to succeed, it was vital to deceive the Germans about when and where the invasion force would land - and Popov was about to play a leading part.

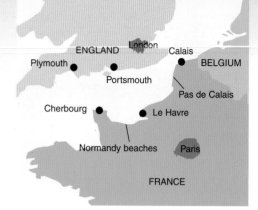

American troops prepare to land at Omaha Beach, Normandy on 6 June 1944. The Normandy landings were the largest naval invasion ever, involving almost three million troops

The Allied intelligence strategy was to trick the Germans into believing that the invasion force would land in the Pas de Calais. The real target was the Normandy beaches

Troops and vehicles coming ashore following the successful assault on the Normany beaches. After D-Day, the battle for Normandy continued for more than two months, ending with the liberation of Paris

Taken by surprise

In the weeks leading up to the invasion, Popov fed information to the Germans that was deliberately designed to mislead them into expecting an attack in the Pas de Calais, rather than Normandy *(see map)*. Other German agents - also working for the British - confirmed his reports. Meanwhile, MI5 made sure that, while the Germans were told of troop movements in other areas of England, no sightings were reported in the south-west, where the main invasion force would actually be launched.

When D-Day arrived, the Germans were taken completely by surprise. The deception was so successful that even after the landings in Normandy had begun, they still believed the real attack would come at Pas de Calais.

Operation Fortitude

Popov's deliberate misleading of the Germans was part of one of the largest and most successful deception operations in the history of military espionage. Codenamed Operation Fortitude, it also involved transmitting faked **signals traffic** and using entire 'dummy armies' of decoy tanks *(below)*, aircraft and landing craft to trick enemy spy planes.

The decoy army of fake tanks and aircraft on the East Anglian coast diverted the Germans' attention from the real invasion force which was about to be launched from the south-west

Looking back on his life as a spy, Popov wrote, "To survive the multiple hazards of espionage it is better not to be too serious... I never took myself or other people too seriously."

'Loyal' to the last

Throughout the war, Popov's cover as a double agent remained intact. The Germans were so convinced of his loyalty to them that they described him as their 'best man in England'. Later Popov refused any payment from the British secret service, saying he was happy to work for a country for which he had 'wholehearted admiration' and that his payment from the Germans was enough.

The records of Popov's spying missions were kept secret by the British government until 2002, when 20 files containing hundreds of letters and papers were made public. Although press reports focused on the more colourful details of Popov's life, the files clearly showed what an important part he had played in defeating the Germans.

Tricks of the agent's trade

One of Popov's favourite ways of communicating with his German spymasters was to send them a postcard! Underneath the mundane message on the card, the real message was written in invisible ink.

A microdot camera used by agents of the Russian secret service, the KGB

Popov also sent messages using microdots. His reports were photographed with a special camera which could reduce a whole paragraph to the size of single full stop. The person who received the microdot could read every word of the microdot with the help of a microscope.

Why not try the invisible ink method to send a secret message to a friend:

• Dip the end of a cocktail stick in a glass of lemon juice.

• Use the toothpick to write your message on a piece of paper.

• Tell your friend to iron the paper, and the writing will be magically revealed!

'BLACK LIKE ME'

The undercover journey of John Howard Griffin

Many spies have been masters of disguise, but few have gone to such lengths to change their appearance as investigative journalist John Howard Griffin.

Writer John Howard Griffin (1920–80) was a lifelong campaigner against the race hatred represented by groups such as the Ku Klux Klan (below)

Born and raised in Texas, John Howard Griffin had always been angered and sickened by the hostility and prejudice shown towards black people in America's southern states. In 1959 he came up with a remarkable plan to expose the real extent of racial injustice in America: he would change the colour of his skin and actually *become* an African American.

The racist Ku Klux Klan flourished in America during the 1950s and 60s and is still active in parts of America to this day. Klan members in white robes often took part in horrifying attacks on black people, including bombings, burnings and lynchings

'Turn me into a negro*'

Griffin knew that in order to write about racial prejudice, it was not enough just to observe it: he had to experience it. He needed to see the world through black eyes and to feel what black people felt. But how could he ever experience racial hatred and intolerance without being black himself?

After making some enquiries, Griffin found a doctor in New Orleans specializing in skin treatment and approached him with a very strange request - 'Turn me into a negro.' Taken aback at first, the doctor agreed to give Griffin a drug that, combined with **ultraviolet** treatment, would darken his skin. Since Griffin's hair was straight and not curly like most African Americans, he wore it as short as possible. After four or five days of intensive treatment, his disguise was complete, and Griffin took to the streets for the first time as a black man.

* The terms 'negro' and 'colored' were widely used in the 1950s and 60s to describe an African American person. They are now regarded as derogatory.

Griffin disguised as an African American. In order to change the colour of his skin, Griffin took regular doses of the drug Oxsoralen, and spent 15 hours a day under an ultraviolet lamp

'The transformation was total and shocking. I had expected to see myself disguised, but this was something else. I was imprisoned in the flesh of an utter stranger... All traces of the John Griffin I had been were wiped from existence.'

John Howard Griffin, *Black Like Me* (1961)

Under the so-called 'Jim Crow' laws which had been introduced in 1876, black people in the southern and border states of the USA were guaranteed 'separate but equal' status. In fact, **segregation** led to conditions that were almost always worse for the blacks. Black people were excluded from decent schools, denied the vote and condemned to lives of poverty. Violence against black people was also common, yet attacks by sinister racist organizations such as the Ku Klux Klan were rarely reported, let alone investigated by the police.

Above: The southern states of America, through which Griffin travelled.
Below: Signs enforcing racial segregation in America in the 1950s

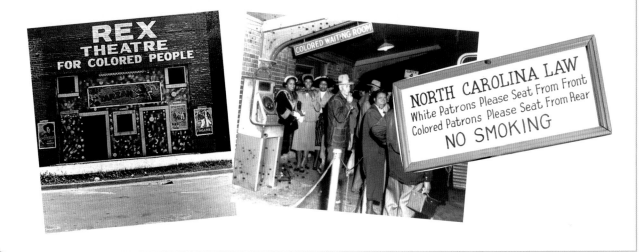

Undercover in the Deep South

During his travels, Griffin made it a rule that if asked who he was or what he was doing, he would tell the truth. In the beginning, he decided to talk as little as possible in order to blend into his new role and surroundings. He was amazed to find that many people who knew him as a white man were completely taken in by his disguise. Even the shoeshine man in his neighbourhood, whom Griffin spoke to frequently, looked at him without any sign of recognition.

Third-class citizen

In his six-week-long travels through Louisiana, Mississippi, Alabama and Georgia, Griffin soon learned what it felt like to be treated as a third-class citizen. He was shocked by what he found. He was turned away from restaurants, banned from rest rooms (public toilets), denied work, forced to walk miles just for a glass of water - all because of the colour of his skin. One foreman told him: 'We're getting you people weeded out from the better jobs at this plant. Pretty soon the only jobs you can get here are the ones no white man would have.'

White Patrons Please Seat From Front
Colored Patrons Please Seat From Rear

"*My skin was dark. That was sufficient reason for them to deny me those rights and freedoms without which life loses its significance and becomes a matter of little more than animal survival.*"

Griffin, *Black Like Me*

Towards the end of his journey, Griffin was sickened by the hatred that he had seen and eager to get back to the life he had known. With his experiences still fresh in his mind, he sat down to write his story. Soon articles by him were appearing regularly in *Sepia*, a magazine devoted to civil rights issues.

Death threats

As his story became public, Griffin began to receive death threats. He and his family were forced to move to Mexico following a violent demonstration in his hometown in which his effigy was hanged. A cross was burned on the lawn of the black church near his home. Despite this, Griffin finished his story and *Black Like Me* was published in 1961. It became one of the most influential books of the day and was published in 13 languages. Griffin spent the rest of his life fighting for civil rights.

Could YOU be an undercover reporter?

Could YOU survive weeks in disguise, travelling from one place to the next, away from friends, family and home comforts? How would it feel to be turned away from bars and stared at because of the colour of your skin?

In his book, Griffin describes how it was only when walking the streets at night-time that he felt safe from the 'hate stares, the contempt'. Why do you think this was?

OPERATION OVERFLIGHT

Gary Powers and the U-2 spyplane affair

When World War II ended in 1945, Europe was divided. To the East lay the communist world of Soviet Russia and its satellite states. To the West, supported by the USA, were the capitalist nations. As both sides looked for ever more sophisticated ways to spy on each other, a new and sinister game of Cold War espionage began.

Spy in the sky

One vital new weapon in the intelligence war was the high-flying U-2 spyplane developed in the USA. Cameras mounted in the plane could provide amazing views of objects on the ground - in some cases, as small as a single car or truck.

When the first U-2 spyplane was launched in 1955 it was hailed by the American Central Intelligence Agency (CIA) as a major breakthrough. A spyplane that could fly over enemy airspace without being detected could gather intelligence more quickly and easily than any agent on the ground.

Formed in 1947, the CIA had the task of collecting and analyzing foreign intelligence. Its deadly adversary was the KGB, the feared Russian Committee of State Security

Non-aligned countries

NATO countries

Warsaw Pact countries

NORWAY
FINLAND
North Sea
SWEDEN
DENMARK
Baltic Sea
USSR
UNITED KINGDOM
REPUBLIC OF IRELAND
NETHERLANDS
EAST GERMANY
POLAND
CZECHOSLOVAKIA
BELGIUM
WEST GERMANY
FRANCE
SWITZERLAND
AUSTRIA
HUNGARY
ROMANIA
YUGOSLAVIA
BULGARIA
ITALY
ALBANIA
PORTUGAL
SPAIN
GREECE
TURKEY
Mediterranean Sea

*During the **Cold War** most countries signed pacts to help defend their neighbours. Warsaw Pact countries sided with the Soviet Union (USSR). NATO (North Atlantic Treaty Organization) countries were allied with the USA. Spain joined NATO in 1982*

Huge wingspan made the U-2 unstable in crosswinds and difficult to land

The U–2 cockpit was not pressurized – the pilot had to wear a pressure suit and breathe through an oxygen mask

Lightweight construction increased the U–2's flying range

The U-2 spy plane could fly at a height of more than 21,300 m. It was equipped with a camera that could take pictures from over 18,000 m. A self-destruct mechanism could destroy the camera and film if the plane fell into enemy hands

One man who was keen to test the potential of the U-2 for himself was US pilot Gary Powers. Born in Jenkins, Kentucky, Powers had joined the United States Air Force in 1950 and had quickly proved to be an outstanding pilot. When the CIA approached him to join the spyplane programme in 1956, Powers accepted eagerly.

On 1 May 1960, U-2 pilot Gary Powers took off from Peshawar, Pakistan, on a top-secret mission to photograph weapons-manufacturing sites in the Sverdlovsk and Plesetsk regions of the Soviet Union. Crossing the border, Powers could see no sign of enemy activity. But what he did not know as he flew deeper into Russian airspace was that his U-2 spyplane had already been detected by the Soviet air-defence system and was being tracked by enemy fighters.

U-2 pilot Gary Powers, pictured here as an Airforce Reserve

Shot down in flames

At first, the extreme height at which Powers was flying made it impossible for the Soviet fighters to intercept him. But eventually an SA-2 Guideline missile fired from the ground came close enough to the U-2 to cripple it. Badly damaged, the U-2 crashed near Sverdlovsk. Powers parachuted to safety, but was immediately captured by Soviet troops and taken for questioning. Hidden in his clothes was the suicide pin issued to all U-2 pilots for use in an emergency. Whether Powers had no time to activate it or chose not to, is not known.

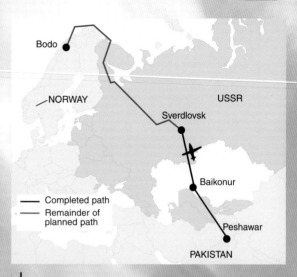

Completed path
Remainder of planned path

The flight plan of the U-2 showing Powers' route from Peshawar in Pakistan to Bodo in Norway. When shot down, Powers was deep in Soviet airspace

Powers' U-2 spylane plunges to earth, streaming smoke and flame from its crippled wing. Moments later, Powers pressed the 'eject' button and parachuted clear before being captured by Soviet ground troops

'One of our spyplanes is missing'

Back in the USA, the loss of the U-2 spyplane sparked a major crisis. Unaware that the pilot had been taken alive and that key parts of the plane had been recovered, President Eisenhower immediately sent out orders to cover up the nature of the mission. A statement was released by NASA claiming that the plane had been a 'weather research aircraft', which had strayed off course when the pilot experienced 'breathing difficulties'.

It was a claim the Soviets could easily disprove. To the embarrassment of the US, Powers was publicly tried in Moscow, found guilty of spying and sentenced to ten years' imprisonment. However, in 1962, after serving only two years, Powers was exchanged for captured Soviet spy Rudolph Abel. He returned to the US and began work again as a test pilot for the U-2. He died in 1977 in a helicopter crash.

Above: A Soviet propaganda photo showing local people inspecting the wreckage of the crashed U-2

Below left: Gary Powers displays a model of the U-2 spyplane while testifying before a US Senate Select Committee after his release by the Russians in 1962

What would YOU do?

After his release, Gary Powers was asked by interviewers how high he was flying when his U-2 was shot down by the Russians. 'Not high enough' was his answer.

During press interviews, Powers was criticized for allowing key equipment on board the U-2 to fall into enemy hands, and for not using his 'suicide pin'. Is this fair?

What would YOU have done?

Glossary

Allied countries led by Britain and America which joined forces to oppose Nazi Germany

codes and ciphers special sequences of numbers, letters or symbols which allow secret messages to be exchanged without being understood by other people

counterfeiting illegal copying of coins and banknotes

Croix de Guerre medal dating back to World War I awarded by the French government for bravery in wartime

double agent a spy who pretends to work for one side while secretly passing information to the enemy

FBI short for Federal Bureau of Investigation, the main US law enforcement agency

fingerprinting taking an inked impression of the unique pattern of skin on a person's fingertips

Geneva Convention(s) treaties dating back to 1863 which protect the rights of soldiers and people who are taken prisoner during wartime.

George Cross medal created in 1946 by King George VI for British civilians who show outstanding bravery. The medal was originally given for acts of courage during the wartime bombing of London.

Gestapo short for Geheime Staats Polizei, the feared secret police of the German Nazis

infiltrate to gain a position of trust inside an organisation or country while secretly working for the other side

intelligence secret information about the enemy

'Jim Crow' laws discriminatory racial laws enforced between 1876 and 1965 in parts of the USA

Maquis another term for the French Resistance

MI5 the part of the British secret service responsible for intelligence operations on British soil

Morse code special 'alphabet' of short and long signals allowing messages to be transmitted by **telegraph** or radio.

mugshot a head-and-shoulders portrait or photograph of a criminal or suspect, usually taken from the front and the side

neutral not fighting on either side during a war or conflict

OBE short for Order of the British Empire, an award for outstanding achievement

Resistance (French) underground organization which fought to liberate France from German occupation during World War II

sabotage blowing up or destroying bridges, roads, factories and army buildings or equipment

segregation physically separating people of different race or background

shadow (vb) to track a person's movements without being seen

signals traffic exchange of radio messages

Special Operations Executive (SOE) secret organization created in Britain at the start of World War II for training agents to carry out sabotage and subversion in Europe

spymaster person who controls the activities of a spy

subversion organizing and stirring up resistance to an occupying army during wartime

telegraph system of electric wires used for sending and receiving messages before the days of the telephone

ultraviolet (UV) light which cannot be seen by the human eye but which can be used to produce special chemical reactions – for example, to treat skin complaints

wiretapping stealing information by intercepting private messages sent by telegraph

Index

Webfinder

The Pinkerton National Detective Agency
http://www.legendsofamerica.com/WE-Pinkertons.html
http://www.loc.gov/loc/lcib/0006/pink.html

Violette Szabo
http://www.violette-szabo-museum.co.uk/

Dusan 'Dusko' Popov
http://news.bbc.co.uk/1/hi/uk/1973962.stm

John Howard Griffin
http://www.hrc.utexas.edu/research/fa/griffen.html
http://www.aamdallas.org/sepia.htm

Gary Powers and the U-2 spyplane
http://aerostories.free.fr/powers/page2.html
http://www.nasm.si.edu/research/aero/aircraft/lockheed_u2.htm